THE ORIGINS & FUTURES OF THE CREATIVE CITY

BY CHARLES LANDRY

First published by Comedia in the UK in 2012
Copyright © Charles Landry

ISBN: 978-1-908777-00-3

Comedia
The Round, Bournes Green
Near Stroud, GL6 7NL, UK

Book design: **www.hillsdesign.co.uk**
All photographs: **Charles Landry**
Cover photograph: *The 'green wall', part of the Quai Branly Museum, Paris.*

This and other Comedia publications are available from:
www.charleslandry.com

Amsterdam: New buildings feeding off the old style plus they mirror each other in reverse order.

CONTENTS

London: Great creative places have great streets - Regent Street.

SUMMARY

These short publications seek briefly to encapsulate key agendas and thought movements that are shaping the city today and have an impact on the future. *The Origins and Futures of the Creative City* sets the platform for a series of other 'shorts' including, *The Sensory Landscape of Cities, The Art of Conviviality, The Digital Revolution & City Evolution, Eco-urbanity & the New Global Citizen, The Creative City Index: Measuring Your Urban Pulse, The Management of Fragility: Cities in the 21st Century.*

The city faces an escalating crisis that cannot be solved by a 'business as usual' approach, including the challenge of living together with great diversity and difference, addressing the sustainability agenda, rethinking its role and purpose to survive well economically, culturally and socially and to manage increasing complexity. These are some of the future priorities for creativity. Creativity needs to address the issues that really matter globally.

Curiosity, imagination and creativity are the pre-conditions for inventions and innovations to develop as well as to solve intractable urban problems and to create interesting opportunities.

Unleashing the creativity of citizens, organizations and the city is an empowering process. It harnesses potential and is a vital resource. It is a new form of capital and a currency in its own right.

Creativity has broad-based implications and applications in all spheres of life. It is not only the domain of artists or those working in the creative economy or scientists, though they are important. It includes too, social innovators, interesting bureaucrats or anyone who can solve problems in unusual ways.

Cities need to create the conditions for people to think, plan and act with imagination.

A crucial challenge is how cities make their invisible creative attributes visible in their physical environment as well as how the city feels. Here the ability to communicate iconically is key.

The city faces an escalating crisis that cannot be solved by a 'business as usual' approach.

SETTING THE SCENE

Some people think we talk too much about creativity, others say its value is only beginning to be recognized. It is astonishing how creativity has moved up global agendas at a rapid pace affecting how we value individuals, assess companies and how desirable we think cities and regions are.

Globally nearly 100 cities call themselves a 'creative city', yet often they only refer to their strong arts and cultural infrastructure. Another instance is the much referenced IBM 2010 Global CEO Study. It concludes that creativity (60%) is the most important leadership quality for success, outweighing even integrity (52%) and global thinking (38%). The study is the largest known sample of one-on-one CEO interviews, with over 1,500 corporate heads and public sector leaders across 60 nations and 33 industries polled on what drives them in managing their organizations today. Depending on your view, creativity is a crucial resource or a vital weapon.

There is, however, a 'creativity crisis' even though creativity is increasingly legitimized. The best-known evidence is the long term Ted Schwarzrock study tracing 300,000 US children through their life, some for 50 years. Its conclusion is that since 1990 creativity is declining.

Contentious & compelling

The creative city concept has become contentious. A danger is that the notion is becoming empty and hollowed out through overuse. Some worry it is too fashionable, thoughtlessly applied without detailed understanding of its potential. Consequently people get bored and think about the 'next big thing': 'the learning city', 'the liveable city' or 'the smart city'. Simultaneously there is a paradox – the more we discuss creativity the more we focus on a culture of risk aversion.

There is a proliferating global frenzy, as places want to evolve as creative cities or simply to claim they are a 'creative city'. Some talk of a Creative City Movement. Everyone is responding to a

Bologna: With new technology we can now work anywhere.

world that has changed dramatically. It feels like a paradigm shift and whilst many things seem the same, their underlying operating dynamics are different.

The Creative City notion seems like an answer to coping with this transition. It is like a rash and has spread everywhere. Often people want creativity to solve more problems than it can cope with. Importantly many problems or opportunities do not necessarily require creativity per se. The central issue is to have a mindset willing to reassess things openly and be creative when necessary.

. A danger is that the creativity notion is becoming empty and hollowed out through overuse.

Some criticize the notion claiming it is only concerned with narrow groups like artists or those in the media, design and performance industries. Whilst both spheres are important the essential question is: what are the specific qualities of artistic creativity that might help establish a more creative city. Equally, impacts of the products, services and the methods of working within the creative economy can make them a significant part of interesting urban development.

Others say the notion simply helps to spectacularize the city to attract the 'creative class', that raft of knowledge workers and researchers who are crucial to developing a more knowledge intensive driven economy. They say this reinforces divisions between rich and poor, taking away the focus from the less privileged, rather than looking at their entrenched problems in an imaginative way. Whilst this segment of the population is crucial, representing perhaps 25% to 30% in a country's centrally located cities, they do not represent the totality of a city's creative forces.

The over-strong emphasis on this group is unfortunate and narrow. Urban creativity is much more. I have stressed: 'what can the other 75% of apparently 'non-creative' people contribute to a more creative city that discovers imaginative opportunities to moving forward or inventive solutions to problems'. To be an urban success I argued, in 1995, that: "Cities have one crucial resource – their people. Human cleverness, desires, motivations, imagination and creativity are replacing location, natural resources and market access as urban resources. The creativity of those who live in and run cities will determine future success. Of course this has always been critical to cities' ability to survive and adapt. Cities, when they became large and

complex enough to present problems of urban management, became laboratories to develop the solutions – technological, conceptual and social – to their problems of growth and change."

The key priorities for creativity today are to create the 4th clean, green, lean industrial revolution, intercultural understanding, help reduce the rich-poor divide and to create ambition and meaning beyond consumerism.

My first Creative City project was in Glasgow in 1989 and called: 'Glasgow – The Creative City & its Cultural Economy'. This signalled an on-going interest in how going with the grain of the culture of a place and its embedded resources can help reinvent a city, its public sector, community organizations and private companies, so as to give it strategic advantage. Since then I have developed my ideas by practically working with several dozen cities and visiting countless others, as well as being inspired by other practitioners and authors.

Cities have one crucial resource – their people.

The primary conclusions are that the creative capacity of a place, is shaped by its history, its culture, its physical setting and its overall operating conditions. This determines its character and 'mindset'. I evolved a contrast between the 'urban engineering paradigm' of city development focused on hardware, with 'creative city making' which emphasizes how we need to understand the hardware and software simultaneously. Today, the essential element of the personality of many cities is their 'culture of engineering', which is reflected in their mentality. The attributes to foster creativity associated with this mindset are both positive and negative. It is logical, rational and technologically adept, it learns by doing, it tends to advance step-by-step and through trial and error. It is hardware focused. It gets things done. There is a weakness, in that this mindset can become narrow, unimaginative and inflexible and forget the software aspect, which is concerned with how a place feels, its capacity to foster interactions and to develop and harness skill and talent. Mindsets, either foster or hinder and block, creative potential. The challenge therefore is to embed an understanding of the soft and creative thinking into how a city operates. Developing a 'creativity platform' is a main strategic tool in establishing a comprehensive 'creative ecology' within a city.

... a 'creativity platform' is a main strategic tool in establishing a comprehensive 'creative ecology' within a city.

More speedily we have moved through phases where the dominance of a particular asset has changed and is highlighted. Another way of expressing it is that our economies and the social life built around them were first factor-driven, then efficiency-driven, and now innovation-driven. Each implies a growing level of complexity.

A cautionary note is crucial. The severe danger in constantly emphasizing innovation is that we develop them for their own sake without any real purpose. They may have little utility nor deal with important needs. The aim is simply to pump up desires by dreaming up ever changing fashions and trends. We should, of course, generate new solutions to many challenges, yet at times the creative response may well be to hold back and to ask ourselves 'do we need this particular innovation'.

London is a hub for fairs. They are a vital element in circulating cultural products.

CRAFTS COUNCIL FORTY 1971–2011
SEE & BUY UNIQUE
CONTEMPORARY CRAFT
FROM 200 MAKERS
CERAMICS, FASHION ACCESSORIES, FURNITURE,
GLASS, INTERIORS, KNITWEAR, METALWORK,
MILLINERY, NON-PRECIOUS JEWELLERY, PAPER,
PRECIOUS JEWELLERY, WOOD, WOVEN TEXTILES
Origin
The Contemporary
Craft Fair
Thurs 22—Wed 28 September 2011
www.originuk.org
TENT EXHIBITIONS
ARTS COUNCIL ENGLAND
square pie
Origin
The Contemporary
Craft Fair
← ENTRANCE
Thurs 22—Wed 28 September
LIBERTY

WAVES OF CHANGE

A curve shows the movement over time from the agrarian to the creativity driven economy. We were primarily an agrarian society for millennia, an industrial one for 200 years, a society whose wealth creation was largely driven by the value created by information for 30 years, we now talk of the knowledge and innovation-driven economies and increasingly one driven by creativity.

Each metaphor such as 'the innovation economy' or 'the creativity-driven economy' provides a helpful lens from which to understand and gauge the shift in the primary means of wealth creation, the basis of competition, the social and cultural priorities, management style and operating systems, the role of the public sector and the measurement of success or failure. Now we have reached a stage where creativity and the capacity to imagine is seen as key.

Every shift in the means of economic wealth creation creates a new social order, new ways of learning and things to learn, new settings in which learning takes places and the demand for new kinds of facilities. It requires different cultural capabilities. For instance, looking at the economy the capabilities and requirements to set up a Ford Motor Company or a Walmart are different from those to create an Apple or a Google or a Kaos Pilots educational centre in Denmark or a Forum Virium in Helsinki.

The 'innovation or knowledge economy', for instance, is largely associated with technological innovation and the skills, attitudes and qualities of technologists, software engineers and other engineering skills or scientifically-oriented people. Without wishing to fall into clichés the personality characteristics of these groups is more logical, linear, rational, analytical and systematic and they of course have elements of creativity as well, but might be less adept at social issues or communication. Surveys, for instance, show that engineers need to pay greater attention to interpersonal skills, communicative abilities and cultural literacy.

There was a level of predictability about the foreseeable results of the former phases. Predicting exactly the 'emerging advantage'

Berlin: Clever piece of art outside a museum with Einstein's formula.

from creativity will be less easy. We are moving from 'managing the known', to a design and innovation approach, that is 'building the unknown'. Yet what is possible is to build capability and encourage the mindset for communities to have the foresight to identify the 'advantage' when it starts to emerge, and so to have the creative capacity to respond accordingly. This requires a governance ethos, management and learning system aware of these needs and willing to adapt to these new demands.

These transitions are not smooth and there are winners and losers. Cities that claim to be creative have many poor people in them and are often badly run. So the scope of creativity must be comprehensive and include creative solutions to social issues and management. Creativity is not only about the arts or sectors such as film, music or design, although they may have special contributions to make.

The knowledge intensive economy

Slowly and with gathering force from the 1960's onwards it became clear that Western societies were changing profoundly. Authors such as Fritz Machlup, Peter Drucker, Alain Touraine and Daniel Bell discussed the coming of a post-industrial society based less on muscle power and more on brain power and its resulting knowledge. A list of key texts is appended. Of course, the industrial era required knowledge, but the difference with the emerging era was its self-conscious use. A series of interlocking issues and common themes highlighted were: Information industries will rise in importance; knowledge is a vital form of capital and an economic resource; science based industries will drive the economy; new ideas can grow the economy; this evolving economy is information and knowledge-led and service-oriented, with a shift from manufacturing to services.

The raw materials of the new system are increasingly information, knowledge and creativity.

The raw materials of this new system are increasingly information, knowledge and creativity. Knowledge here is both a product and a tool to enhance the value of other activities. Rather like with good food you need both ingredients and a recipe which is knowledge. (Romer). Knowledge is the next level up from information, since through judgement and analysis it adds value to any idea, product or service. Yet the analysis of information can have vast impacts such as how live information helped the logistics industry create just-in-time production processes. Knowledge is essentially

human capital, accentuating the different skills and workers needed to run society. In a more knowledge intensive economy, the specialized labour force is maths and computer literate and data savvy. Knowledge is difficult to pin down, but entails subject and technical expertise and the intellectual capacity to problem-solve and discover opportunities. Companies always seek to etch any knowledge into their own processes and products so that it cannot escape with those who hold it. Knowledge can grow rather than deplete by being shared and applied. This shifts the economy from scarcity to potential abundance. Allied is the global reach enabled by computing power, the new media, creating collective intelligence via connectivity and interactivity and vastly easier access to knowledge sources. A characteristic is the speed of transaction and agility of processes. Knowledge-enhanced products or services are more expensive than those with low embedded knowledge. Strong communication abilities are vital to make knowledge flow, affecting social structures and cultural setting of organizations and cities.

The impacts of the evolving knowledge intensive economy were dramatic on the organization of work and cities. The deindustrialization process in the West reduced the power of blue-collar workers and their unions, with a rise of professional workers and the 'creative' professions associated with design or new media. Regretfully, there are always winners and losers in these dramatic transformations. Remember, and this is hard to believe, that we thought that cities had little hope, as cities hollowed out as industries declined and moved production to Asia and elsewhere. New York, as one example, nearly went bankrupt in the 1970's.

The resurgence of the city

This significant phenomenon emerged in the transition to knowledge intensity from the early 1980's onwards. The city began again to exert a gravitational pull, because of its resources in learning, its capacity to help exchange and transactions, its cultural institutions and richer artistic life and vibrancy, its stock of buildings and infrastructure and its transport links. The city was seen as an accelerator of opportunity. The city is a dense communications system that is not easy to replicate in other settings. Once the urban focus re-emerged a vast urban regeneration process began with the tearing down of the past to make the city ready for professional service-related industries, offices and residential developments that frequently pushed out older tenants as a result of the gentrification process. Often the results were negative. Simultaneously an extensive retrofitting exercise began. Worldwide several hundred old warehouses, breweries; train, bus or fire stations; cement, coal, textile, tobacco or steel factories; old markets or military barracks were transformed into culture or experience centres, incubators and company breeding grounds and as hubs for wider urban regeneration. The creative professionals in particular were drawn to these places. It is strange that those same places that had horrible working conditions began to be celebrated as places for the new and the hip. Why do these structures resonate? They exude memory and the patina of ages, in an age where novelty increasingly erases memory and of course, physically their spaces are large and allow for flexibility and interesting structures.

The city was seen as an accelerator of opportunity.

Examples include most famously those in the Ruhr such as Zeche Zollverein in Essen or Duisburg Landschafts Park, the Distillery District in Toronto, the Cable Factory in Helsinki, Halles De Schaerbeek in Brussels, the Custard Factory in Birmingham, the refurbishment of old industrial buildings in Pyrmont Ultimo in Sydney, Metelkovo in Ljubljana, the Truman Brewery area around Brick Lane in London and many, many more.

At the same time many people could not find a role in this evolving economy, their skillset did not fit, which led in many places, in Allen Scott's words, to 'surface glitter and its underlying squalor'.

The Ruhr area once Europe's major industrial hub is transforming dramatically.

THE TRAJECTORY OF THE ORIGINAL IDEA

The idea of the Creative City, as contrasted to the 'creative milieu', emerged from the late 1980's onwards along a number of trajectories. When introduced in the late 1980's[1] it was seen as aspirational; a clarion call to encourage open-mindedness and imagination. Its intent was to have a dramatic impact on organizational culture.

The philosophy was that there is always more potential in any place than any of us would think at first sight, even though very few cities - perhaps London, New York, Amsterdam or Berlin - have been comprehensively creative over time.

It posits that conditions need to be created for people to think, plan and act with imagination in harnessing opportunities or addressing seemingly intractable urban problems. These might range from addressing homelessness, to creating wealth or enhancing the visual environment. It is a positive concept; its assumption is that ordinary people can make the extra-ordinary happen if given the chance. This agenda was also part of the democratization and empowerment process that was steadily making headway in the same period.

Creativity in this context is applied imagination using qualities such as intelligence, inventiveness and learning along the way. In the 'Creative City' it is not only artists and those involved in the creative economy that are creative, although they can play crucial roles. Creativity can come from any source including anyone who addresses issues in an inventive way, be it a social worker, a businessperson, a scientist or public servant. It advocates the need for a culture of creativity to be embedded into how the urban stakeholders operate. Encouraging creativity and legitimising the use of imagination within the public, private and community

Malaga: has reinvented its city centre to foster human interaction, exchange and transaction.

[1]See Landry Charles, Glasgow: *The Creative City & its Cultural Economy*. 1990, Glasgow Development Agency; Landry and Bianchini, *The Creative City*. 1995, Demos, London; Landry Charles, *The Creative City: A Toolkit for Urban Innovators*. 2000, Earthscan, London.

Creativity ...
is applied
imagination
using qualities
like intelligence,
inventiveness
and learning
along the way.

spheres will broaden the ideas-bank of possibilities and potential solutions to any urban problem. This is the divergent thinking that generates multiple options, which needs to been aligned to convergent thinking that narrows down possibilities from which urban innovations can then emerge, once they have passed the reality checker.

This requires infrastructures beyond the hardware – buildings, roads or sewage. Creative infrastructure is a combination of the hard and the soft, including the mental infrastructure, the way a city approaches opportunities and problems; the environmental conditions it creates to generate an atmosphere and the enabling devices it fosters, generated through its incentives and regulatory structures. It requires thousands of changes in mindset, creating the conditions for people to become agents of change rather than victims of change, seeing transformation as a lived experience not a one-off event.

The built environment – the stage, the setting, the container – is crucial for establishing a milieu. The industrial city and its milieu looks, feels, operates and uses resources differently from a knowledge intensive or creative city. The latter needs a different physical environment, which fosters sociability, exchange and mixing, in order to maximize its potential. In this way it becomes an accelerator of opportunities.

It needs to provide the physical pre-conditions or platform upon which the activity base or atmosphere of a city can develop. A 'creative milieu' is a place that contains the necessary requirements in terms of 'hard' and 'soft' infrastructure to generate a flow of ideas and inventions. A milieu can be a building, a street or an area, such as Truman's Brewery in Brick Lane, London, Rundle Street East in Adelaide, Queen Street in Toronto and Soho in New York.

Becoming and being a creative city is very much concerned with changing mind-sets, it is more a process than a plan, it is dynamic not static. There is no fixed point at which a city is creative. To maintain a creative position a city needs to be continually alert and strategically agile.

London: The creative industries like design and music are one of the drivers of the new economy.

Cultural resources

Today creativity is seen as being applied to any field, but in the late 1980's when most of the constituent ideas were developed the key terms discussed were: culture, the arts, cultural planning, cultural resources and the cultural industries. This was because people began to recognize that a new economy was emerging and the urban environment was becoming homogenous, dull and dispiriting with similar brand names dominating and that the old fabric of cities was being thoughtlessly destroyed in the name of urban renewal. As a consequence local distinctiveness was declining and eroding.

To fully harness creativity we need to think of resources more widely and draw on the history of places and their culture. In sum, these are cultural resources and are embodied in peoples' creativity, skills and talents. They are not only 'things' like buildings, but also symbols, activities and the repertoire of local products in crafts, manufacturing and services. They are the raw materials of the city and its value base; its assets replacing coal or steel. Creativity is the method of exploiting these resources and helping them grow. A city region has a vast array of these raw materials. They include: Unique resources embedded in peoples' inventiveness, skills and talents. The natural setting; the weather, topography, water and created landscapes, such as parks. There are natural resources such as coal and forests; history, heritage

> To harness creativity we need to think of resources more widely ...

An appreciation of culture should shape the technicalities of urban planning ...

and tradition in the built fabric, in memories and rituals, and in acquired skills. It encompasses the quality of overall design, the pattern of streets and neighbourhoods, the balance between good ordinary buildings, the spectacular and iconic and representative structures. It consists of infrastructures from IT to transport as well as how a city does its urban housekeeping. It contains specialist local industries and services and the skills and talent base as well as research and educational possibilities. Increasingly too, the capacity within the cultural industries is important from design to new media or film and the performance sectors. Furthermore, it involves activities cutting across trade fairs, sports, the artistic arena and those that are community based, as well as festivals and events. Finally, attitudes and attributes can be assets, such as whether there is a culture of curiosity or organizational competence.

Even the resulting regulations and incentives regime can act as a creative stimulus. For example, it is possible to use taxation in ways that encourage certain initiatives or behaviours.

The task of urban planners is to recognize, manage and exploit these resources responsibly. An appreciation of culture should shape the technicalities of urban planning and development rather than being seen as a marginal add-on to be considered once the important planning questions like housing, transport and land-use have been dealt with. A culturally informed perspective should condition how a city thinks of itself and its vision for the future, as culture helps us understand where a place comes from, why it is like it is now and how this might determine its potential. This focus draws attention to the distinctive, the unique and the special in any place.

The creative (cultural) industries

The creative industries, formerly called cultural industries, such as music, media, performance or design were important in pushing the creative city agenda forward and from the late 1970's onwards UNESCO[2] and the Council of Europe had began to investigate the sector. From the perspective of cities it was Nick Garnham, an

[2]*UNESCO Cultural Industries: A challenge for the future of culture*, 1982, UNESCO, Paris.
[3]Enzensberger Hans Magnus, *Raids and Reconstructions*, 1976, Pluto Press, London.
[4]Landry Charles, Bianchini Franco, Ebert Ralph, Gnad Fritz, Kunzmann Klaus, *The Creative City in Britain and Germany*, 1996, Anglo-German Foundation.

academic at the Greater London Council in 1983/4 who put the cultural industries on the wider urban agenda. Drawing on, re-reading and adapting the original work by Theodor Adorno and Walter Benjamin in the 1930's which had seen 'the culture industry' as a kind of monster, and influenced too by Hans Magnus Enzensberger[3] he saw the cultural industries as a potentially liberating force. Garnham felt that whilst the alternative media movement, which had been a strong oppositional force in the 1970's, was important it tended to marginalize itself and speak to itself. Furthermore, he was concerned that many of these activities were based on sweated labour and self-exploitation or reliant on grant funding. Instead, he argued that focusing on commercial viability, the market and real audiences, had positive benefits and potentially would have far greater impact on changing the media landscape.

Over time as cities such as Liverpool, Sheffield, Manchester or Birmingham struggle with industrial restructuring, the cultural industries seemed a possible answer to a mixed conundrum of problems, such as the need for new jobs, how to anchor identity in a changing world, how to foster social inclusion. When the Labour government returned in 1997 the Department of Culture, Media and Sports renamed the cultural industries the creative industries, perhaps trying to avoid its political connotations, and set up a Creative Industries Task Force. Meanwhile, within European cities similar developments began to take place although with a time lapse that has now been overcome. Equally the recognition of the importance of the sector came late to the European Union with the first comprehensive assessment of the sector in 2001 called 'Exploitation and Development of the Job Potential in the Cultural Sector in the Age of Digitalisation'.

Comedia, my organization founded in 1978, was a player in this development, undertaking studies in London, Birmingham, Barcelona and others in the mid- to late-1980's. The first detailed study of the creative city concept was, 'Glasgow: The Creative City and its Cultural Economy' in 1990, this was followed in 1994 by a meeting in Glasgow of 5 German and 5 British cities (Cologne, Dresden, Unna, Essen, Karlsruhe and Bristol, Glasgow, Huddersfield, Leicester and Milton Keynes) to explore urban creativity, resulting in *The Creative City in Britain and Germany*[4], followed by a short version of *The Creative City* in 1995 and a far longer one called *The Creative City: A Toolkit for Urban Innovators* in 2000, which popularized the concept.

The talent agenda

Cities began to compete more intensely with each other from the late 1980's onwards and an alignment developed between the knowledge and creativity agendas. This created a focus on the human resources needed to make the city competitive. Steve Hankin from McKinsey coined the term 'war for talent' in 1997, which is shorthand for the skill, expertise and human potential a city needs to compete. Here people began to ask what are the physical, social and cultural conditions needed to keep and attract skilled people,

Cities began to compete more intensely with each other from the late 1980's.

especially those with strong reputations who have choices where and with whom they wish to work. They are the primary resource of an organization. Talent, is a vague term and the talent required will depend on context, such as whether one is working in the public, private or community sector. In one case you might want an interesting entrepreneur, in another a good hospital manager or leader of the transport department and in a third you might require a social innovator. Some characteristics though can be identified and they seem to include being strategically alert, a willingness and capacity to lead, to have emotional intelligence and to communicate well, thus to think well and to be able to deliver.

The appearance of Richard Florida's book, *The Rise of the Creative Class* in 2002 hit a nerve and reinforced the talent agenda with its clever slogans such as 'talent, technology, tolerance - the 3T's' and interesting sounding indicators like the 'gay index', that could give numbers to ideas. Importantly it connected the three areas: a creative class - a novel idea, the creative economy and what conditions in cities attract the creative class. At its core Florida argues that a new sector has emerged in communities - the 'creative class' - those employed in coming up with new ideas and better ways of doing things. Places with large numbers of creative class members were also affluent and growing he argued. To support his theory, Florida identified occupations he considered to be in the creative class, and to measure their size and composition. Companies are attracted to places where creative people reside argued Florida and he found a strong correlation between places that are tolerant and diverse, as measured by his Gay and Bohemian indices, and economic growth. He concluded that economic development is driven in large measure by lifestyle factors, such as tolerance and diversity, urban infrastructure and entertainment.

Dubai: The city has attempted to blast itself into global consciousness, often in the strangest ways.

QUALITIES & CHARACTERISTICS

Creativity has a general, all-purpose problem-solving and opportunity-creating capacity. Its essence is a multifaceted resourcefulness and the ability to assess and find one's way to solutions for intractable, unexpected, unusual problems or circumstances.

Equally it helps a process of discovery through the supple capacity to imagine possibilities, to conceive and originate concepts and ideas and downstream to help bring them into being. In this way it enables potential to unfold. It is applied imagination using qualities such as intelligence, inventiveness and reflexive learning along the way. It is valuable in the social, political, organizational and cultural field as well as in technology and the economy. It can be applied to all spheres: from rethinking schools and teaching, inventing new systems of healthcare and delivery, recasting organizational structures. Crucially, it is now recognized that creative inputs add value to businesses that are not normally considered creative, such as engineering, facilities management or the hospitality industry as distinct from design, film or music. Creativity is generic, a way of thinking and a mindset, and it has specific applications and is task oriented in relation to particular fields.

Creativity requires certain qualities of mind, dispositions and attitudes. These characteristics include: curiosity, openness and a questioning attitude, the ability to stand back, listen and re-assess, the courage not to take a given credo, practice or theory for granted and to dare to think outside the box, the gift of seeing relevance and connections between apparently different things. It involves fluency and flexibility and the ability to draw on ideas from across disciplines and fields of inquiry, to think laterally and to blend concepts from seemingly unrelated domains. It is based on divergent thinking, which opens out possibilities, reveals patterns and helps find solutions before prematurely closing in on a specific answer.

Creativity is not only concerned with the new or a loose openness. To be effective in being creative means having the judgement and knowing when to be flexible and open and when to be more

Shanghai: The World Expo in Shanghai 2010 had the theme 'Better Cities, Better Life' with cities around the globe presenting their credentials.

27

focused and closed or tenacious and persistent. A misconception is that being creative is about being unconstrained. Being creative requires just as much attention as being a scientist or an engineer. The central point is that it is a different kind of attentiveness and approach. So in terms of education, as an instance, creative learners need four key qualities: to identify new problems, rather than depending on others to define them; to transfer knowledge from one context to another; to treat learning as an incremental process, in which repeated attempts will eventually lead to success; and to pursue a goal. The range of skills required include: self-organisation; being inter-disciplinary and to have personal and interpersonal abilities.

Creativity requires certain qualities of mind, dispositions and attitudes.

Everyone, is in principle creative, but not everyone is equally creative, yet everyone can be more creative than they currently are. The same applies to organizations, neighbourhoods and city regions. Some aspects of creativity can be learnt but many individuals or organizations have default ways of thinking. Some flourish in a more free ranging context, others find it threatening and destabilizing. It seems that most people and organizations prefer the comfort zone of the tried and tested, the known and apparently proven.

Creative behaviour and the ability to innovate occurs when two types of mind are present. One is the exploratory, opportunity seeking and connecting mind that can range horizontally across facts, issues and specialist knowledge and detect threads, themes and cross-cutting agendas. This is the enabling mind associated with being creative. This needs to be allied to the focused, vertical mind of someone who knows a topic, subject or discipline in profound detail. This is the instrumental mind.

Individual, organizational & urban creativity

We can grasp quite easily what a creative individual might be like; for instance their capacity to make interesting connections, to think out of the box or recast established theories and to have sparks of insight. They have energy and courage as well as some sense of where they are going, although it is often unclear how they are going to get there. The same is true for a creative organization. But already the priorities are different and it adds a layer of complexity and a different dynamic takes place.

Madrid: Wherever you look there is always imagination bursting to come out.

A creative organization probably has mavericks and creative individuals, but for the organization to work it needs other types too: Consolidators, sceptics, solidifiers, balancers, people with people skills. Some people consider these types as less interesting, but that is dangerous, because for the creative organization to work it needs mixed teams. How teams work together becomes significant. You need to achieve a series of balances, such as between being collaborative internally and perhaps using external competition to push you forward. And the organization needs a story and a proposed trajectory to give itself purpose in an attempt to make itself more internally cohesive. The task is to align internally to face an outside world. Indeed it may be the case that a creative organization has quite 'ordinary' people in it, but because its spirit or ethos is open, exploratory and supportive this maximizes potential. This may then lead to greater, sustained organizational achievements. This often happens in sport where a team with no supremely gifted individuals wins, because it knows better how to make the most of its parts. The key is its open ethos. The value of ethos is incalculable.

In the creative city ... complexity rises exponentially ...

Moving on to the next layer – the creative city – issues become very difficult as complexity rises exponentially as you involve a mass of individuals and an amalgam of organizations with different cultures, aims and attitudes. These can push in opposing directions. For example, it may be that some are pushing for urban expansion and extension, whereas others focusing on the sustainability agenda want to densify things. Or one organization may display great cultural understanding, whereas another may basically not get it. The challenge then is to discover where the lines of strong agreement can flow and to build on these so that similarities become more important than differences.

The Creative City notion does not imply there is a cosy consensus.

The Creative City notion does not imply there is a cosy consensus. Instead it stresses how rules of engagement between differences can be negotiated to move forward as in a mediation process. The overarching skill needed for a creative city, therefore, is that of the connectors, enablers, and facilitators. These can be individuals or intermediary organizations who can stand above the nitty-gritty of the day-to-day, important as this is, and look at what really matters.

'What really matters' in a city depends on circumstance. In one instance it may be to help stop young people leaving the city by harnessing their potential more effectively, in another to address ecological issues and in a third to deal with social clashes between groups in a neighbourhood. Yet, increasingly what matters, and this makes things extremely hard, is being 'creative' itself: that is 'providing the pre-conditions to think, plan and act creatively'. This means organizations changing their work culture.

In other words, we are only at the beginning of the 'creative city' journey. The notion has not embedded itself into the genetic code of key institutions that make up cities.

Edinburgh: An interesting sign above a shop selling telescopes. It encapsulates symbolically the creative city agenda.

A CREATIVE PLACE

To plan a creative city we need to know what it is like. A creative place can be a room, a building, a street, a neighbourhood and a creative city or a city-region is a good amalgam of all these. Their qualities are similar: A sense of comfort and familiarity, a good blending of the old and new, variety and choice and a balance between the calm and invigorating, or risk and caution.

People feel they can fulfil and express themselves and harness their talents for the overall good; there are opportunities. These talents act as a catalyst and role model to develop and attract further talent. There are myriad, high-quality learning opportunities, formal and informal. Self-development is easy, learning programmes are forward looking, adaptable and highly connected. There are ladders of opportunity and choices and a sense that ambition and aspirations can be met. There is a 'can do' mentality. The city is an engine of possibilities.

There are places to meet, talk, mix, exchange and play. There is multicultural colour and diversity, as this implies distinctiveness and varied insights. It is an 'intercultural' place, where the focus is on mixing different cultures and experiences and sharing ideas and projects together.

The confidence to be outward looking comes from a sense of familiarity with people around them and the physical landmarks in the city, be that a street, a café or a set of facilities. This anchors their sense of safety and security. The feeling of an evolving, adaptable community is important. Once people have confidence they want to explore, be curious and surprised. This creative place exudes crucially a sense of a 'higher purpose'. It has soulful places, perhaps a gallery or a site of interest – a kind of cathedral of the post-industrial age.

The overall physical environment functions well, it is easy to move around and connect. The architecture, old and new, is well assembled, and the street pattern is diverse and interesting. It generates pride. Webbed within the ordinary is the occasional extraordinary and remarkable. Creators of all kinds are content,

Amsterdam: The new business district Zuidas is trying to attract global knowledge nomads yet appeal to the locals.

but not complacent, and motivated to create and communicate their work. People exchange ideas, develop joint projects, trade their products, or work in its advanced industries. It offers a rich register of vibrant experiences such as food, the arts, heritage and nature, including thriving mainstream and alternative scenes. The place is welcoming and encouraging. Its dynamism makes it a magnet and so generates critical mass and attracts people from outside.

Its political and public framework has purpose and direction. It understands the importance of harnessing the potential of its people. Its workings are focused, easy to navigate and accessible, open and it encourages participation. Public employees get things done regardless of departmental boundaries. Differences are debated, accepted, negotiated and resolved without rancour. Its leadership has vision and is strategically agile yet is grounded in day-to-day reality. It is respected and trusted and recognizes its vital role in continuously identifying new opportunities. It fosters cohesion, is relatively open to incomers and to new, even uncomfortable ideas. Creative places are often not cosy and can be edgy. This place enjoys being a creative hub and its physical environment. Levels of crime are in general low, the place feels safe and standards of living are relatively high. It is socially alert and seeks to avoid ghettoizing its poorest. Social organizations are active, well-funded and constructive.

Industry is innovative and design aware, with a strong focus on new trends, emerging technologies and fledgling sectors such as developing the green economy or creative industries. It is networked and connected and its commitment to research and development is above average. Cross-fertilization, across even the most diverse sectors occurs naturally. Public private partnerships happen as a matter of course. The business community is entrepreneurial, has drive and is forward thinking. It understands and utilizes its natural resources well, it harnesses existing talents and acts as a breeding ground for new skills. Business leaders are respected figures and give something back. The community in turn is proud of their products and the reputation they bring. It has effective communications systems including local and international transport, high-speed internet access and connectivity to the world at large.

Overall, this place is unlike any other. You sense the buzz, it is obvious to residents and visitors alike. It accentuates its distinctiveness in a relaxed and unthreatening way. It is at ease with itself. Its history, culture and traditions are alive, receptive to influence and change, absorbing new ideas which in turn evolve and develop its distinctiveness and culture.

Portugalete: A creative response to topography, making it easy to negotiate hills in the Bilbao Estuary town.

THE SHIFTING GLOBAL LANDSCAPE

The city region in transition

The creativity notion has moved centre-stage, so we can talk of a movement. There are many triggers and these include: The fierce nature of urban competition and because the old ways of doing many things no longer works. Globally over the last 20 years, cities have been searching for answers to re-establishing their purpose and creating new kinds of jobs, whilst their cities were physically often locked into their industrial past. This led to soul searching and meant re-assessing the old ways and many concluded, to take two instances that: Education did not seem to prepare people for the demands of the 'new' world; they remained factories to drill-in knowledge rather than communities of enquiry; they taught specific things rather than acquiring higher order skills, such as learning how to learn, to create, to discover, innovate, problem solve and self-assess. This means talent was not sufficiently unleashed, explored and harnessed. Second, hierarchical management systems in the public and private sectors were recognized as not efficient in a world where flatter, networked structures showed greater promise and new business models such as 'open innovation' were emerging.

Every city of ambition wants to get on the global radar screen.

In sum the world of cities and regions has changed dramatically over the last 20 years and the reinvention of places like the Ruhr, Bilbao, Helsinki, Melbourne, Chicago, Vancouver, Hong Kong, Kuala Lumpur or Sao Paolo is emblematic of this shift. Cities of every size in every location face periods of deep transition largely brought about by the vigour of renewed globalization and changes in the world's urban hierarchy. Each city-region needs to reassess its role in this new configuration as they need to move their economy to one based on greater knowledge intensity.

Every city-region of real ambition wants to move up the value chain and capture centrality for itself. This is why city-regions are continuously searching to be global niche centres of significance. The overall aim of these ambitious places is to increase their 'drawing power', by whatever means. This assesses the dynamics of attraction, retention and leakage of power, resources and

Helsinki: New economy companies like Nokia seek to create open physical environments that encourage creativity.

talent. The right blend makes a city attractive and desirable with different aspects tempting different audiences: Power brokers, investors, industrialists, shoppers, tourists, property developers, thought leaders. Overall this creates the resonance of a city. Few places manage to develop the integrated and sophisticated city marketing that brings these elements together. Melbourne, Amsterdam and Berlin do it well. The consequence of achieving drawing power shows itself in economic, political and cultural power – the ability to shape things – and thus performance and wealth. New dimensions of competition are emerging, such as being 'green' and here places like Zurich, Freiburg and Copenhagen have made a significant impact.

> The aim of ambitious places is to increase their 'drawing power'.

Cities now compete by harnessing every dimension of their asset base and practically all the major global city-region players have recognized 'creativity' as a new multifaceted resource. Many have creativity strategies such as Singapore, Amsterdam, Berlin, Shanghai, London, Hong Kong, Osaka or Toronto. Increasingly too, second- and third-tier cities like Ghent are following in their wake.

Making the invisible visible

The resources city regions can creatively use can be hard, material, tangible or soft, immaterial, intangible, they can be real and visible or symbolic and invisible, they can be countable, quantifiable and calculable or to do with perceptions and images. Ambitious cities seek to project and orchestrate their assets 'iconically'. The aim is to pull attention to the city, to create a richness of association and recognition and to grab profile. Icons are projects or initiatives that are powerfully self-explanatory, jolt the imagination, surprise, challenge, and raise expectations. You grasp it in one. In time they become instantly recognisable and emblematic. Very few of these exist and the newest is likely to be the Elbphilharmonie in the HafenCity Hamburg designed by Herzog de Meuron. Others that have caught the imagination include the Palm in Dubai. Most memorable are the physical ones. An icon, however, can be tangible or intangible: A building, an activity, a tradition, having a headquarters of a key organization in the city, the association of a person with a city, a plan or an event like the Olympics can be iconic. A city can even be iconic when it has many associations, like Paris, New York or Istanbul, that build upon each other into

a powerful composite picture. Most importantly images and perceptions need to be grounded in reality.

There is a battle as to how to measure the significance of places, as our measurement systems for assessing city dynamics are often out of date. We measure static quantities, such as population or gross domestic product, usually derived from the Census, as important as these are, as distinct from relational measures, such as the power or information flows, connections, linkages, reputation, iconic presence and other less tangible factors. This is why a whole new raft of indicators and ranking systems have been proposed.

... the world of cities and regions has changed dramatically over the last 20 years.

THE DYNAMICS OF CREATIVITY

Creativity: A resource & currency

For the first time in history, the imagination of the mind ... is the primary source of economic productivity and problem solving.

The implication is that today there is a premium on creativity. For the first time in history, the imagination of the mind and its resulting knowledge is the primary source of economic productivity and problem solving. We have evolved from a world where prosperity depended on natural advantage (arising from access to more plentiful and cheap natural resources and labour) to a world where prosperity depends on creative advantage, arising from being able to use and mobilize brainpower to innovate in areas of specialised capability more effectively than other places.

Success depends on a city's capacity to identify, nurture, harness, support, promote and orchestrate and mobilize its creative resources. It needs to develop its 'creative ecology'.

Critical mass & size

Creativity potential is determined by context. These factors are often beyond the control of a city. They include the physical location, the geography, the size of the place, national politics or levels of centralization. Critical mass is key in achieving certain aims. Historically it was usually the larger places that became renowned for being creative. Looking at the acknowledged creative places from the past it is striking how many of them were hubs of empires, such as Athens, Vienna or London or the centre of trading routes or entry points like Venice or New York. Unsurprisingly, as poles of attraction they lured the best and the brightest from around their known worlds, which continually helped reinforce their positions, so helping to generate the cultural and political power as well as complex specialisms or industrial clusters through which they created their wealth.

Each of these famous creative hubs offered us something unique from which we can still learn today. Athens gave us an intellectual heritage that fostered debate, analysis and critique. Venice highlights to us the importance of specialization, expertise and trade networks. Florence reminds us how important new business models are such as its invention of banking systems.

Bilbao: The city's urban renaissance is globally recognized, blending the playful and the functional. Jeff Koon's famous 'Puppy' in front of the Guggenheim.

Brisbane: Festivals of ideas are increasingly becoming popular as people search for new answers to the world's problems.

Vienna shows us how a configuration of core ideas can affect a number of disciplines simultaneously. The rise of Paris as an arts and fashion leader was triggered and aided by royal sponsorship, which is in effect public investment. London in the swinging 1960's hit a global Zeitgeist or mood of change and the success of San Francisco's Silicon Valley helps point out the elements required, organizational, financial and legal, to turn ideas into reality.

The interesting question is whether smaller places, especially those with industrial traditions, such as producing coal, steel, manufactured goods or beer, can be creative. In relative terms the answer is yes. Whilst they cannot compete with global hubs, there is a vast range of global niches and strengths to be captured. And indeed, very large places often become dysfunctional and so reduce their creativity potential.

The need for creativity should be seen in the light of new complex problems ...

What appears to be important, are the forms of expertise that are agglomerated in a particular place. Here the idea of the quinary sector is helpful. The traditional breakdown of primary, secondary and the tertiary or service sector are well-known. Yet the tertiary sector is immense and includes activities that are vastly different. Being a waiter or hairdresser is a service job, but cannot really be compared to being a lawyer or software engineer, which require different intellectual attributes. Some therefore define this as the quartenary sector. The quinary sector includes activities involving

Istanbul: A stark cultural clash – a shop with naked mannequins next to a mosque

the highest levels of decision-making and strategic thinking and planning, where often ideas, concepts, models and products and services are rethought and reinvented. The creative city has a higher proportion of these people.

Urgency & wicked problems

The need for creativity should be seen in the light of new complex problems, such as greening and sustainability, which if treated seriously, will need to reshape how we think and behave. Some refer to this as the rise of wicked problems. Many public policy problems, such as obesity, which cut across health and social issues, are severely complex. Called 'wicked problems', they are seemingly intractable, made up of inter-related dilemmas, issues and interweave political, economic and social questions. Wicked problems cannot be tackled by traditional approaches where problems are simply defined, analysed and solved in sequential steps. They have characteristics that make traditional hierarchical, top-down thinking less adept at solving them. There is no definite or unique 'correct' view of formulating the problem; and different stakeholders see the problem

and solutions differently, often with deeply held ideological views. Data is frequently uncertain, difficult to acquire or missing. They are connected to other problems and every solution reveals new aspects of the problem that needs adjusting.

The greatest impact of creativity comes when it finds a way of solving wicked problems.

Cost disease

The particular challenge is for the public sector to keep and attract talented people. The relative wages between the public and private sector are under pressure. This is because of the 'cost disease'. Many activities especially within advanced manufacturing can increase productivity dramatically through IT improvements or inventiveness and therefore justify salary increases. Making more with less is effectiveness in these contexts. In services and personalized services, which is largely the domain of the public sector, productivity increases by contrast are more difficult to achieve. If a teacher increases their productivity by having classes of 20 rather than 10 we deem this to be a loss of service. The same applies to a nurse or a social worker dealing with more patients or clients. Yet, their relative skill and wage expectations are the same as those working in advanced manufacturing. This upward cost pressure is the cost disease. For the public sector there are few choices. They will inevitably have higher salary demands and probably lower investment. This means the public domain needs to be open to new and innovative ways of operating. It has to be imaginative in re-inventing services in order to make its resources work harder.

Settings & milieu

Creativity needs physical and organizational environments, settings and a management ethos that encourages it to happen. Many organizations, institutions or cultures inadvertently kill their creativity by 'crushing' their employees, or in the case of education their pupils' intrinsic motivation – the strong internal desire to do something based on passions and interests. Environments, firms or places, that encourage individuals or organizations to become creative have a number of features, including: giving people the freedom and authority to act by delegating authority; presenting

Creativity needs physical and organizational environments, settings and a management ethos that encourages it to happen.

the right scope of challenge that is achievable but stretches people enough; providing sufficient time, human and financial resources to allow for trial and error as well as to make mistakes; creating a supportive team context where people are committed to the project, to each other and where ideas and different opinions can be shared to develop the potential of an idea, process or product; managerial and organisational support by creating an environment that publicly values and rewards creativity. Clearly this impacts on how companies, schools, universities or city-regions operate.

A new organizational ethos is shaping up. It differs from the more simplistic efficiency and effectiveness paradigm associated with the late 20th century. The characteristics and operating dynamics of the progressive early 21st century corporate or public bureaucracy include being resourceful, strategically agile, responsive and imaginative.

The applications of creativity are context driven. In the 19th century it was, for instance, the creativity of scientists in discovering the cure for cholera that advanced public health. In the 20th century those that invented computers ultimately created the Internet-based economy. In the 21st century two focuses for creativity are essential. The first is needed to advance the fourth lean, clean, green industrial revolution as well as to solve the problems of social integration or conviviality or rethink healthcare and social services. The second is the ability to think holistically and across disciplines. In part, this requires people to think differently because then they do things differently and ultimately, perhaps different things.

Creativity & the bureaucracy

One arena for creative action is the public bureaucracy, as the 21st century version will need to be different from and solve more complex problems than the public bureaucracy of the 20th century. Our Western bureaucracies were developed to address issues of their time and reflect the culture of their age. At their best they sought systematic procedures to bring transparency, fairness and equity to decision making. Yet as they evolved weaknesses appeared and combined with managerialism they became convoluted. Changes are already afoot in the organisational practices of the public sector, commercial companies and in the wider world. It includes a shift to involving users more and co-creating policies, products or solutions; a shift from hierarchical, to network thinking, a breakdown in traditional disciplinary boundaries, and cultural cross-fertilization. These have implications for how bureaucracies need to operate. The 'creative bureaucracy' idea is not a plan, but a proposed way of operating that helps create better plans and better ways of operating in the future. It is an adaptive, responsive and collaborative organisational form that in principle can harness the initiative, motivation and full intelligences of those working in them and respond to the changing demands of those they seek to serve.

The Creative City Index

In order to measure and monitor the creative pulse of a city my colleague Jonathan Hyams and I have developed a 'creative city index' focusing on 10 domains under which there is a raft of assessment questions and groups of indicators, which will be described in greater detail in another Comedia Short in this series.

These are:

Political & public framework

Distinctiveness, diversity, vitality & expression

Openness, tolerance & accessibility

Entrepreneurship, exploration & innovation

Strategic agility, leadership & vision

Talent development & the learning landscape

Communication, connectivity & networking

The place & placemaking

Liveability & well-being

Professionalism & effectiveness

While the 10 domain headings generally speak for themselves one would look for a strong showing in the following qualities: Motivation, tenacity, awareness, clarity of communication, broad thinking, inspiration, aspiration, adaptability, dynamism, openness, participation, design awareness, sensory appreciation, professional pride, leadership, vision. An assessment of creativity should focus on the education and training system, industry and business, the public administration and public bodies, the community and voluntary sector, the culture, tourism and leisure domain.

It is possible to measure the creative capacity of a city.

Berlin: Urban development always involves battles to blend well the old and the new.

THE COMPETITIVE PLATFORMS FOR AMBITIOUS CREATIVE CITIES

City regions with the right strategic focus can punch above their weight in spite of global dynamics, but a series of factors are important. In essence they act as a road map for urban creativity.

Urban leadership

The first of these is leadership and the six main qualities of urban leadership seem to be: Foresight, which is the ability to imagine and vision and to assess how deeper trends will play themselves out. Strategic focus, the skill of concentrating on the 'big picture' and long-term future-oriented perspectives and within this the ability to be strategically principled and tactically flexible. There is a need to understand urbanism, city dynamics and iconics in a holistic way and the qualities and characteristics that make cities great. Framing this knowledge, a culture of openness and curiosity is essential, which involves adopting an ethos which values debate, critical thinking and learning. In order then to make things happen organizational agility is important, which is the ability to move from a controlling, centralizing, uniform, high blame, low risk culture, to one which values responsiveness and flexibility. Yet this quality needs to be allied to a determined delivery focus, which is the motivation, will and ability to make what is promised happen – to 'walk the talk'.

An ethical development perspective

Values driven development has become more important. This is partly driven by ethics and also self-interest thus merging the self-centred with the public good. This is because there is a profound yearning especially among the highly educated under-40s, which all aspirant creative cities want to attract, to give back to society or the world. This important shift I describe in the book, *The Art of City Making* where I discuss the need for cities to strive 'to be the most creative cities for the world' rather than 'to be the most creative cities in the world'. This one change of word

Malmo Western Harbour: Is a carbon neutral development it combines an icon with ordinary apartments.

*... be the most
creative city
'for the world'
rather than
'in the world'.*

- from 'in' to 'for' – has dramatic implications for its operating dynamics. It gives city-making an ethical foundation. It helps the aim of cities becoming places of solidarity where the relations between the individual, the group, outsiders to the city and the planet are in better alignment. This means environmental and social justice issues rise to the fore. If cities want to attract the talented from the world this cannot be avoided. Indeed companies are increasingly driving the climate change agenda for mixed motives, but especially to keep an incoming flow of the most talented people.

The same logic applies to city-regions that want to be seen as leaders and role models, who therefore take global responsibilities especially in relation to sustainability issues. See how Singapore, London and soon New York have instituted congestion charging or Stockholm and Copenhagen have taken a lead on the environment. Even China is hitting the green road.

A consequence is that cities are attempting increasingly to bend the market through rethinking their regulatory and incentives regime to address imbalances. Social justice issues such as affordable housing become more significant as a creative city needs also to be liveable for all social groups. Many cities like London demand a social housing component for key workers, such as nurses and the police, in all their major developments. This reduces commuting times and helps efficiency of the city dramatically.

Integrated thinking, planning & acting

The complexity of cities cannot be addressed through 'silo thinking' or departmentalism. Specialisms still matter, but they need to be framed within a mindset that recognizes how things are inextricably interwoven. It is difficult to see the whole by moving up from the parts. Yet in reverse it is easier to understand the detail, having seen the interconnections and interdependencies.

At the highest level there needs to be a conceptual shift and thus the overarching paradigm for urban development would change from an urban engineering or infrastructure-driven approach to creative city making. This is the art of making places for people, including the connections between people and places, movement

*Osaka Dotontori area: Is this creative
or simply shouting too much?*

and urban form, nature, and the built fabric, and the processes of building successful settlements. This involves the ability to combine hardware and software initiatives. How the physical city is put together in the creative city-making context now needs to serve social relations and networking dynamics. Cities must now understand the value of the latter emphasizing issues like atmospherics, liveability, well-being and the value and values of public realm.

At a more day-to-day level in the creative city many things are redefined, reconceived and operated. Even simply renaming can have dramatic longer-term effects, as what we choose to call things determines how we think about them and the priorities we set. The transport department, for instance, may be renamed and subsumed under a mobility and accessibility division, which is concerned as much with pedestrians as with cars or metro systems. Or waste or sewage issues may become part of a resource management system as new ecological thinking turns waste into an asset.

... the overarching paradigm changes from an urban engineering, or infrastructure driven approach, to creative city making.

Strong concepts can change perspectives especially when they force us to think horizontally and vertically at the same time. 'Seamless connectivity', for instance, seeks to ensure all transactions happen without friction or difficulty. This has not only a physical dimension, such as enhancing mobility so you can walk from A to B, or whether neighbourhoods easily connect and congestion and traffic jams are reduced. It also has economic and social dimensions. Here we ask 'how easy is it to transact and to get things done', are the bureaucracies responsive, effective and flexible? Do immigration procedures work speedily? Do regulations encourage networking and transactions? Is IT connectivity ever present? How many meetings can I have in a day?

Ultimately this implies rethinking governance for 21st century needs, including the appropriate regulations and incentives structures that are strategically principled and tactically flexible. This involves too, blending public, private and community driven approaches, whilst ensuring that their best attributes are maintained, cherished and valued. In addition, unfortunately, city management has many blind spots since it is usually organized along traditional functional lines, such as housing, parks, health, police or transportation. Other dimensions, which may be the things that 'really matter'; such as responsibility for the overall atmosphere or social networking and bonding are often no-one's responsibility.

Future-proofing & resilience

Cities that are punching above their weight including Bilbao, Barcelona, Helsinki, Melbourne and Singapore all have practical, long-term think-tank organizations focusing on the 30 year horizon and they constantly monitor the best initiatives in the world and try to go beyond them. Only benchmarking against the best is being a follower not a leader. This includes the capacity for high-level conceptual thinking and strategic planning to stay well ahead of trends. A useful metaphor is to see this as 'a collective thinking brain' for the city.

Only benchmarking against the best is being a follower not a leader.

The aim is to future-proof the city and to make it resilient. When this perspective is embedded into forward planning it reflects the ability to imagine the implications of shallow and deeper trends and how these might play themselves out. It requires investing in future assets to safeguard against shocks, the unexpected and uncertainty. This helps develop strategic robustness and tactical flexibility.

Are current infrastructure developments, for instance, such as schools or universities, hospitals, police stations or museums being conceived within a future perspective? Schools at times look like factories for drilling in knowledge or hospitals are rarely built to be centres for well-being. If education institutions are reconceived as centres for curiosity and imagination they would look, feel and operate differently. Hospitals conceived as centres for well-being and preventative medicine would too, as would police stations conceived as centres for community engagement.

Knowledge & the learning landscape

The capacity to create knowledge through creativity lies at the heart of the creative city. This implies a varied mesh of formal and informal learning opportunities. This ranges from the obvious such as attracting knowledge and research-generation centres, from universities to science parks. The aim too is to attract

thought leaders in many fields as well as renowned public sector and business leaders who contribute to the creative city with their vast knowledge and experience but may have nothing to do with formal educational set ups. Yet they may, for instance, be part of think-tanks or be involved with them.

But there are many other forms of knowledge creation, exchange and transfer possibilities, which can be encapsulated under the heading 'open innovation'. Indeed many new forms of knowledge required for the creative city will not come out of the traditional learning institutions, since they involve issues like 'enhancing network capacity' or developing new business models. In addition, there are exchange fora such as Pecha Kucha or the First Friday concept, which when managed well can act as accelerators of opportunity and new understandings. Furthermore there is the knowledge required to set up a creative milieu in the first place.

... cities are raising the bar on infrastructure standards as part of overall urban design ...

The focus on identifying, nurturing, harnessing, promoting, attracting and sustaining internal skills and talent as well as drawing these in from outside highlights issues like liveability. A 'CEOs for Cities' survey in the States reports that whereas 15 years ago 80% of educated people chose the company or the job before the city, now 64% of these choose the city rather than the job. The creative knowledge-intensive city has a different look and feel from an industrial city.

This is why cities are raising the bar on infrastructure standards as part of overall urban design, such as airport quality, making public transport a delight to use, giving streets the feel of avenues and boulevards rather than thoroughfares. Great cities are seen less as a series of roads connecting disparate projects, but great streets uniting neighbourhoods and areas. At times too it requires courage and boldness and the ability to conceive of path breaking or audacious initiatives like the Guggenheim in Bilbao or the dramatic retrofitting of recycled buildings.

In the city that encourages learning and exchange, educational institutions should be less like islands operating in isolation but interwoven in multiple ways into the urban fabric.

Hong Kong modernism: A certain beauty but do these buildings attract creativity?

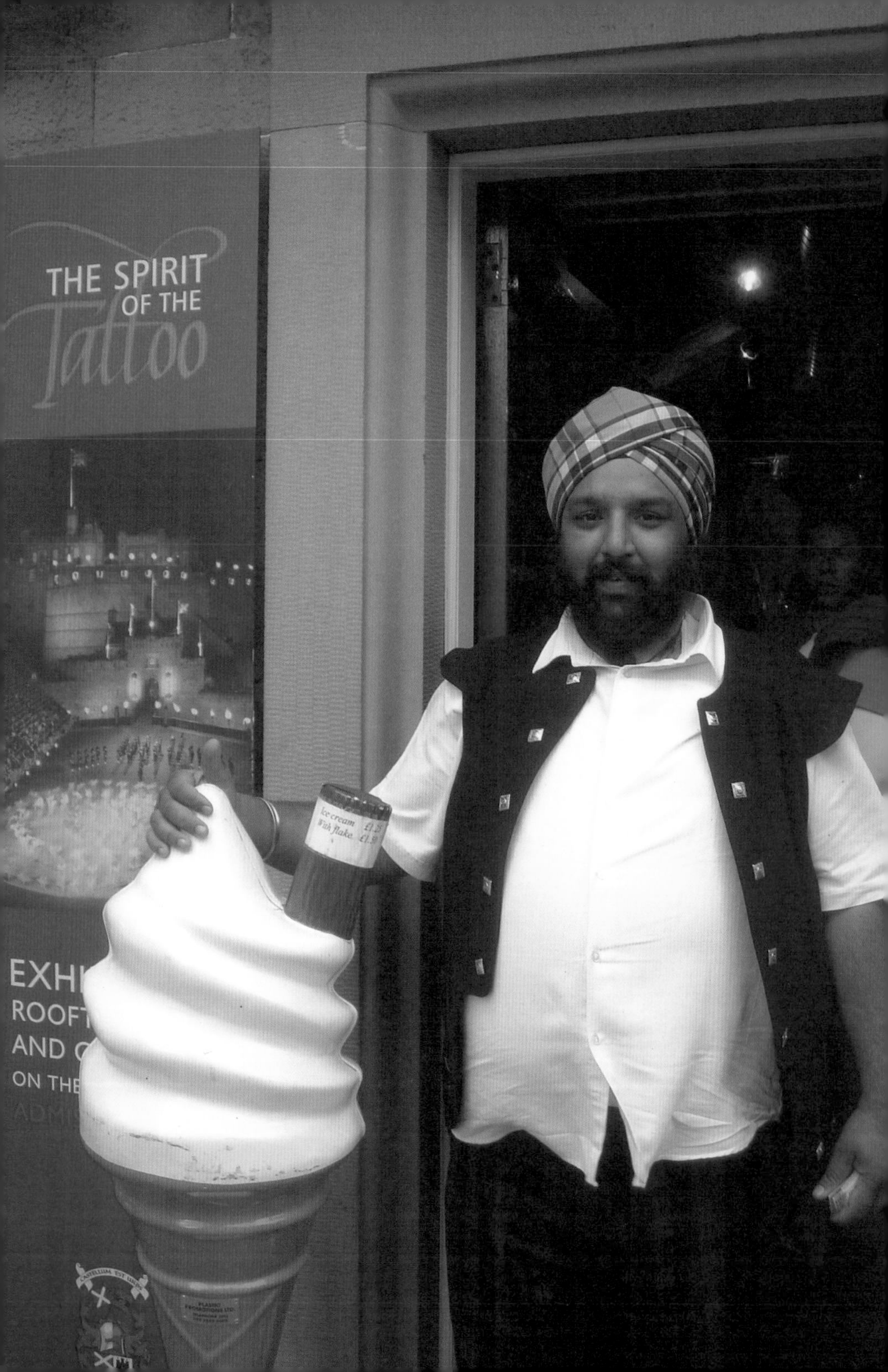
THE SPIRIT OF THE Tattoo
Ice cream
With flake

CONTOURS OF THE NEW

Openness & design thinking

The contours of the new wave are becoming much clearer as the nature and processes of technological innovation are changing and the watchword 'open innovation system' encapsulates this movement. 'Collaborative service design' or 'co-production and co-creation' are other central themes rising in importance. These underlying trends in the development of knowledge intensive economies are evolving at a dramatic pace with user driven product development and co-creation having a particular focus. The development of new IT platforms and web 3.0 with its immersive, interactive, ubiquitous and experiential focus will exacerbate this shift to co-creation. It changes how products and services are conceived and designed and how value added is created. It has implications for both the public and private sectors. The trend for cities to get local people to come up with new ideas for public urban spaces fits this thinking perfectly. Another notion which expresses a deeper trend is the 'experience economy'. It fits the idea that the world is increasingly dominated by 'imagination intensive industries'. Here businesses focus on orchestrating memorable products and events for their customers, which is the 'experience' and sectors such as film, design, music and new media are central in creating these. The danger here is that you simply spectacularize the product or the city.

The mental dispositions and skills to be successful ... include communication ability, collaborative interdisciplinary working, cultural literacy and lateral and holistic thinking.

These trends will have powerful impacts on the desirable qualities in individuals and on the culture of organizations and how they need to work. Private or community sectors and public administrations need to ask themselves whether the skills are sufficiently present. The mental dispositions and skills required to be successful and rising to the fore more strongly include openness, creativity, communication ability, collaborative interdisciplinary working, cultural literacy and lateral and holistic thinking. In organizational terms it means far more integrated working, the capacity to value the combined insights of different disciplines and the need to operate as task-oriented teams as distinct from operating in silos.

Edinburgh: We all have mixed identities. An Indian Scot who owns an Italian ice-cream parlour.

This is not to decry the strengths of the specialist or subject expert, however to make the most of possibilities or to solve complex problems mostly requires the ability to work across boundaries and knowledge domains, especially since the structures and departments we usually operate with come from a period where priorities and the global dynamics were different.

In this context 'design thinking,' as part of the overall creativity paradigm, is seen as instrumental in coping with these shifts. Design thinking involves an ability to combine rationality, creativity with empathy in meeting needs. As a process it 'builds up' ideas and judgments are withheld for as long as possible and thus more ideas and possibilities are generated and fear of failure is reduced. In principle, this can increase lateral thinking and creativity. In contrast analytical thinking, which predominated in the former phase of innovation is more linear and tends to break issues up into component parts in order to understand its essential nature and inner connections and relationships. It is the world of 'who', 'what', 'where', 'when', 'why', 'how'. Without wishing to denigrate these qualities, on their own they will not bring about the solutions to evolving problems or emerging opportunities.

Movements of change

Economies, societies and cultures evolve and new necessities emerge. Four movements over the last 30 years exemplify this: The quality imperative, the added value of design, the need for innovation and now creativity, show the shifting focus in highlighting how organizations, cities and regions can become successful. Together they form part of a new common sense. They are competitive tools. The aim is to embed these attributes into the genetic code of a city. Deeper drivers explain their significance. Quality requires conscientiousness, attention to detail and the maintenance of high standards. The threshold of necessary 'quality' has risen in overall terms. It highlights the ideal of reliability, consistency and predictability and the concept of continuous improvement and just-in-time production. Total quality management highlights the idea of alertness, adaptability and responsiveness. Now it is not simply continuous improvement that is required, but breakthroughs in how people think and solve problems. In the quality paradigm, improvement is regarded as step-by-step or one-dimensional change, while innovation is seen as multidimensional sometimes involving breakthroughs. Delivering a solution that is unique is becoming more important than delivering a standard solution with near perfect quality. The quality of design of the innovation becomes the differentiating factor. Design differentiation creates competitive advantage. Design links functionality and aesthetics. It is a bridge to turn creative ideas into innovations. The desire to generate rich experiences makes good design a prerequisite for success. Firms have always needed to innovate. What has changed is the speed at which they must do so, driven by the pressures of global competition. In addition the scope of innovations has broadened beyond product innovation in private companies to include innovations in the public sphere such as in healthcare or social services or new forms of service delivery or governance.

Alignment & bridging

Creativity and innovation are related. They connect, but crucially they are not the same. First there is a need for curiosity, with which it is possible to be imaginative and from which creativity can emerge. These first steps are divergent. Then, when creativity is assessed, by going through a reality checker, prototypes and inventions can emerge, which if generally applied become an innovation.

Yet the creativity and innovation agendas are aligning, especially in considering how they are to be measured. Innovation thinking has moved from simply focusing on inputs to a systemic approach, as it is clear that, for instance, levels of R&D on their own do not by definition involve creativity or lead to innovations. Wider conditions, namely the creative climate, it is recognized, determine the capacity of a place to be innovative within which specific attributes are necessary components such as good education and skills or research expenditure. Current discussions on innovation indices now include ideas such as 'total innovation' or 'hidden innovation'. This draws attention to how innovation needs to pervade a whole environment.

To capture the dynamics of innovation, analysts talk of a fourth generation of indicators, which stress the interactions and relationships of actors in the innovation system, from firms to universities or public agencies, to the culture, whilst bearing in mind the relative usefulness of formerly popular measures. The development of indicators lags behind how we understand the dynamics of reality. This is why the importance of the culture and creativity agenda was not seen.

A rich urban experience

Most urban experiences are shallow, disappointing and increasingly homogenised. A creative city thus seeks to generate a rich, deep experience, which is not pre-digested and over-branded, where citizens feel they can be makers, shapers and co-creators of their experience rather than merely consumers of the pre-given. This requires the city to be confident in its identity in order to develop cultural depth and sophistication as well as play off and be inspired by its history. Indeed creativity and history are great partners both in terms of the physical fabric, but also the intellectual depth that comes from having a past, which at its best triggers new thinking. Yet crucially a balance is needed. Valuing history, tradition and the tried and tested too much can hold places back. Being alert is essential as the virtues that make places great or successful in the past may be precisely those that help it fail in the future. So a culture of considered and mindful openness is essential.

This richer experience involves combining a strong 'local buzz and global pipelines'. Local authenticity and the soul of a place need to come together with the best of the international. Yet the distinctively local and place-specific and its identity need to be the overarching frame. Linked to this, a good public realm is needed to encourage serendipity

Aberdeen: Simple things like a stool can create a relaxed public space.

so chance encounter, face-to-face contact occur easily and so you can 'bump into the fun' – central requirements to develop the creativity-driven knowledge-intensive economy.

When these things come together well a city can craft its centrality by becoming a transactional hub. This requires rethinking logistics beyond material factors, which is the art and science of managing product and service flows as well as ideas, creativity and knowledge. It helps a city have influence over global strategic networks whether physical, virtual or knowledge and research based.

Pulling these elements together the dynamic and evolving creative city needs to move from brand building to urban reputation management. In marketing, a brand is the symbolic embodiment of all the information connected with a product or service, such as a name, an image, symbol or expectation arising in the minds of people. Yet it is important to focus on tangible achievements rather than hype, as these can encourage a self-reinforcing and self-sustaining cycle of creativity. To be a creative city is an unfolding journey and emergent process, force fed and accelerated by what has already been achieved.

BIBLIOGRAPHY

Bell, Daniel (1973). *The Coming of Post-Industrial Society: A Venture in Social Forecasting*. New York: Basic Books

Drucker, Peter (1969). *The Age of Discontinuity*. New York: Harper & Row

Florida, Richard (2002). *The Rise of the Creative Class: And How it's Transforming Leisure, Community and Everyday Life*. New York: Basic Books

Hall, Sir Peter (1998). *Cities and Civilization: Culture, Innovation and Urban Order*. London: Weidenfeld & Nicholson

Howkins, John (2001). *The Creative Economy: How People Make Money from Ideas*. London: Penguin Books

Kalantzis, Mary and Cope, Bill (2008). *New Learning: Elements of a Science of Education*. Cambridge: Cambridge University Press

Kelly, K. (1999) *New Rules for the New Economy*. London: Fourth Estate

Landry, Charles & Bianchini, Franco (1995). *The Creative City*. Bournes Green, Comedia/Demos

Landry, Charles (2000). *The Creative City: A Toolkit for Urban Innovators*. London: Earthscan

Landry, Charles (2006). *The Art of City-Making*. London: Earthscan

Machlup, Fritz (1962). *The Production and Distribution of Knowledge in the United States*. Princeton: Princeton University Press

Porter, Michael E. (1998). *Clusters and Competition: New Agendas for Companies, Governments and Institutions*. From, *On Competition*. Boston: Harvard Business School Press

Scott, Allan J. *The Resurgent City: Economy, Society and Urbanization in an Interconnected World*. OECD

Seltzer, Kimberley & Bentley, Tom (1999). *The Creative Age: Knowledge and Skills for the New Economy*. London: Demos www.demos.co.uk

Touraine, Alain (1971). *The Post-Industrial Society. Tomorrow's Social History: Classes, Conflicts and Culture in the Programmed Society*. New York: Random House

Wood, Phil & Landry, Charles (2007). *The Intercultural City: Planning for Diversity Advantage*. London: Earthscan

Qingdao: Massive
urbanization is
continuing globally.
Do we yet know
how to make
liveable cities?

CHARLES LANDRY

Speaking, projects & research:

Charles Landry gives tailor-made talks on a wide range of topics, including: 'The Art of Great City Making'; 'Getting your City onto the Global Radar Screen'; 'Beyond the Creative City'; 'Punching Above Your Weight As A Smaller City'; 'Innovative Approaches To Running Complex Cities'; 'Imaginative Examples Of Developing Urban Cultural Resources'; and 'Green Urbanism'. These talks are aimed at a diverse range of audiences from city leaders to urban activists and the business and development community. Charles has recently spoken at events in Sydney, Shanghai, Abu Dhabi, Amsterdam, Milan, Minneapolis and Toronto.

Charles Landry undertakes task-specific projects or research, and acts as a commentator writing articles. He undertakes residencies ranging from one week to three months where a specific challenge or opportunity is worked through and presented publicly at the conclusion. While other projects involve deeper, longer-term relationships with cities and organizations: where strategies are created and tracked, reports are written and meetings chaired and facilitated.

The Creative City Index:

Charles Landry and Jonathan Hyams have developed The Creative City Index. This strategic tool assesses and measures the imaginative pulse of cities. To date, a dozen cities have been assessed including Bilbao, Perth, Canberra, Freiburg, Ghent and Oulu.

Books:

Titles by Charles Landry can be purchased online and from bookshops. Comedia Shorts are also available as e-books. Discounts are offered on bulk orders over 10 books, for events, workshops and meetings. **www.charleslandry.com**.

Contact:

To book Charles Landry as a speaker, to discuss a project and to enquire about The Creative City Index go to: **www.charleslandry.com**

Titles by Charles Landry:

Comedia Shorts 01: *The Origins & Futures of the Creative City*.
ISBN: 978-1-908777-00-3

Comedia Shorts 02: *The Sensory Landscape of Cities*.
ISBN: 978-1-908777-01-0

Comedia Shorts 03: *The Creative City Index*.
ISBN: 978-1-9087770-02-7

The Creative City: A Toolkit for Urban Innovators, Second Edition. Earthscan
ISBN: 978-1-84407-598-0

The Art of City-Making. Earthscan
ISBN: 978-1-84407-245-3

The Intercultural City: Planning for Diversity Advantage. Earthscan
ISBN: 978-1844074365

'City-making is a difficult art and Charles Landry has captured its essence. His world view is valuable to people everywhere who care about cities.'

Carol Coletta, President, CEOs for Cities, USA